# LACHRIMA VECTA

Blake Jerome Everitt

© WILD GOAT PRESS 2019

Printed by Wild Goat Press

Copyright © Blake Everitt

ISBN: 9781794525542

All scripture verses come from William Tyndale's 1526 New Testament

Cover photo by Richard Heaven

For more information:
twitter.com/wild_goat_press

# CONTENTS

| | |
|---|---|
| Alverstone | 8 |
| Alverstone Marshes | 9 |
| Alverstone Manor | 10 |
| Kern Farm | 11 |
| Bowcombe | 13 |
| Bowcombe Down | 14 |
| Chillerton Down | 15 |
| To Our Lady of Whitwell | 16 |
| Brighstone Down | 17 |
| Brighstone Forest | 18 |
| To the wild goats of Coombe Bottom | 19 |
| Culver Down | 21 |
| To the Belgae | 22 |
| Brading | 23 |
| Brading Marshes | 24 |
| Brading Down | 25 |
| Lachrima Vecta | 27 |
| Adgestone | 29 |
| Carisbrooke Castle | 31 |
| Arreton Down | 34 |
| Arreton Church | 35 |
| St. Helens Old Church | 36 |
| Binstead Beach | 37 |
| Quarr Beach | 39 |
| St. Martin's Down | 40 |
| Luccombe Chine | 42 |
| Luccombe Down | 43 |
| Bonchurch Landslip | 46 |
| Bonchurch water spring | 48 |
| St. Boniface Down | 50 |

| | |
|---|---|
| Flowers Brook, Ventnor | 51 |
| Steephill Down | 53 |
| Ventnor Cemetery | 54 |
| Lowtherville | 55 |
| Rew Down | 56 |
| Week Down Barrow Cemetery | 57 |
| Shippards Chine | 62 |
| Apse Wood | 63 |
| Under a bust of Charles I | 64 |
| A cellar in the Paris Belleville fauborg | 65 |
| For Bram van Velde | 66 |
| In an Anglican Churchyard | 70 |
| For Georges Rouault | 71 |
| 'And the angell thrust in his sycle...' | 72 |
| Hymn to solitude | 73 |

PREFACE

These poems delve into the landscape and its history – the deeper layers. Almost all were written outside, at the indicated locations: face to face, feet in soil, open in prayer-trance, knowing its contours, scars, beauty, along with its patience and passion. 'One spends his life, in a spirit of love and humility, deciphering imperfectly Nature and Humanity', as Georges Rouault said. The rest, a small number, were written at my desk whilst contemplating specific sites. Far from academic, merely intellectual, or literary influences, they are scribbled excavations, wandering in subsoil. (For the former read: ruthless careerism, mercenary ethos, hideous commodification of education, and epistemic cannibalism.) They are, like me, poor creatures of 'vyle rayment' (James 2:2), asking for forgiveness always. I love the landscape. I listen and watch in solitude and silence. Miraculously a birth appears: poetry.

Blake Jerome Everitt
January 2019

'For the very creatures shalbe delivered from the bondage off corrupcion, into the glorious libertie off the sonnes of god. For we knowe that every creature groneth with us also, and travayleth in payne even unto this tyme.
Not they only, but even we also which have the first frutes of the sprete morne in ourselves and wayte for the adopcion, and loke for the deliveraunce of oure bodies' – Romans 8:18-23


'Let the brother of lowe degree reioyce in that he is exalted, and the ryche in that he is made lowe. For even as the flower off the grasse shall he vanysshe awaye. The sonne is risen with heate, and the grasse is widdered, and his flower is faulen awaye, and the beautie off the fassion off it is perisshed: even so shall the riche man perisshe in his aboundance' – James 1:9-11


'On the hilles was a voyce herde, mournynge, wepynge, and great lamentacion. Rachel wepynge ffor her children, and wolde not be comforted because they were not' – Matthew 2:18-20

# LACHRIMA VECTA

*Alverstone*

Land and water wed
in scar-sacred lines

bog-void pearling its dark womb
as copper-sewn blight
gnaws itself true;

    oakwings, oakwings
    wait for me there

    as I strain to hear
    that thing so rare:

outgnawing my wordprints
    your fever-shroud echoes
        anointing the causeway.

*Alverstone Marshes*

Mudspear broken
in votive moss

air thickens, unslain,
the frost of wordlungs
sounding deep

the stone-laced gut,
where bogs grow hair
in lieu of soul

and invaders pity not
the troubles they have wrought

*shrammed against the cold.*

*Alverstone Manor*

Who would sever
the poem's roots
      in mines unmanned

by Goibhniu's blade
when time would swirl
      and never land,

proffering its sacred hand
to those that would
      discard it not

as stillborn thresh
haunt's Tovi's rest
      as bark is cleansed

in other airs;
received, once more,
      ancestral peers:

again I ask
why they severed
      your verbclad shoots,

for plant or man
the gods approve.

*Kern Farm*
1
Sandstone
    can words weave
        your muteness?

    Harold's farm
  cleaves its bow
beneath Aissheseye's tombs.

      Daggers sink teeth
        in ploughvoid mess;
        going deeper, the flint knows
      red-orange, oxidised to bless.

    Neolithic vigil maimed,
  rolling succession of gods,
gore-grey, scraping retouched flakes

  as quernstone root-teeth
 guide spoils of soilflower;
Pius' coin left to rot, eyeing its new dawn:

     a ghost-pelt sacrum
   with canine apostles

   sad Saxons sing
 enslave, beneath the weight

 the sorrow of uprooting
 the tremors of Golgotha
where flint gnashed its song.

## 2

Winter's brawn deathlid
    unhoods its steady armour
goading time in legions of clay
    as all will change, stay the same.

    Beech spiders
    its coarse skeleton
    as Wyrd beds the knife intact

    and bloodstraw frees
    its trilling mound;
    waters roll wordlings down
    to grasp abannition.

Reliquaries, tear-forked,
    why does the knee not bend,
the word not cry, as grass-inhumed
    secretions fly and Woden names
    their wooden Christ.

*Bowcombe*

Through coldest grain
the verbploughs drove,
in hail of pain
a hearth once wove.

Subsoil claws the marrow
within, as word-troughs
gild their offers

and topsoil casts the outer din
as Normans fill their coffers;

bark is bled, the *burh* is fled
and layers may lay
their eggs in lairs,

driving verbploughs through coldest grain:

soilclamp of gathered storm
their descendants unearthed your urn

driving wordploughs through coldest grain.

*Bowcombe Down*

Tear-flamed, the pyre sings
of hlawe-womb goods
pried from urn-mask rage

and west-woven decapitations
marry older layers, sewing
breath-bitten Teutonic screed

Cernunnos' people lost
with hare broach pierced
and eyes in Frankish thrones.

Cries surround the barrow,
harp-notes of grief lacing earthflesh,
as bone knows bone another way

than we know: fires, wound-lit,
cannot shed darkness here
where sacrifice is refusal's caress

in dark grey flint.

*Chillerton Down*

The Roman interlude
surges not – as once imagined –
up, but under heft of quern
and claw of cross;

Cain's brood sailing peat of mind,
their god, failing, realigned
with snarling Saxon: ashen rind
the Durotriges' lilting demise.

*Under heft of quern*
*and claw of cross*
*the Briton trickles*
*a bloodied frost.*

*To Our Lady of Whitwell*

The white well
has blackened forth
to leave its shell
for waters drawn

wordmoss tells a tale
stoneswept vaunt

where brothers of low degree rejoice
exalted, and the tear-rich dayfugue
is made low:
                Our Lady of Whitwell
                parsed in stone.

*Brighstone Down*

From the Age of Iron
    you sit in silence
        singing this severed South.

    Grazed by wind and hoof
        your rhythm falls
            keeping guard of spirit-shards;

        Chillerton's fort, urn for mouth,
      risen in dark-roved spine, walks
its drought, for Dian Cécht's harvest

            of blemished herbs

            sighting their eyes
        in selago's sorrow
        as night bathes day
        for renewal.

*Brighstone Forest*

Lugh of the Long Arm
        split my wordlight
        gests in two

revealing a core
        beside which
        their tints fail:

        stricken
    in winter
  for Bright Stone's veil.

*To the wild goats of Coombe Bottom*

1

Bone-stayed, your horns
give grace
to pellets of devastation

lurking glass
of sin's raw cask

time-shreds blackening earth
untouched as you are

traipsing the wordwell's
smeared mercy,
                    solstice-gaunt.

## 2

Teargnawn
the mound's death-ooze
greets

    a lifelong cross;

insects of negation, a loving bite,
or brothels of affirmation

    sty-bright in the muck
    of coil-born silence

there is One who will *not* partake.

*Culver Down*

Another world cups its hands

    Hearth blessed
craft shimmers

    flint alive with toil

    sacred incisions
Tree sparks Mother

    birth inhumed in light

    the dead not far
to stone are turned

    life arrives at dawn

    Presence beneath
a livid tarp

    churning god of storm

    another world cups its hands
graves perspiring beyond

    the reeds creaking home
    *the reeds seeking none.*

*To the Belgae*

Black torques of word-mire
votive heads slicing air
as iron bleeds the shaman's ire
and water boils hearth-sore's glare

sturdy, dissolving

grain-votive, climbing the tracks;

the poem's wingshrouds probe
its sunken abodes;

stricken verbshards, skullstrewn
                          we wait
like neck-rings worn
breath effuscates.

*Brading*

The shale of mind-scur
years breeding bloodsilt
in the rut of Arwald's trough,

still kneading wihtwara
beside the hem of chalk and grass
splaying the wrack of Saint Urien's mast.

Teutonic rite –
reave of rune-void clasp –
rape of veilstrewn craft;

stayed mice of Caedwalla
in Wilfrid's lichen denials
betraying the tracks of iconophiles.

*Brading Marshes*

The marsh trawls its gore;
apostles burning nightly
the deeds of Odin's craft:

esurience the colon's crown,
naked and dead the promise.

*Brading Down*

1

Soilfall sheer
air prays the gulf

between Royalist phlegm
and dire salt;

unhealed soulscabs
biting at deeper wares:

your hand
stills the mindplough
for a minute's scorn,

"*how far you have flown
with this devil's crone.*"

## 2

Avenging lash of chalk
your earthworks split roots
Janus-gaunt.

Barkflensed, birds rue
the age of capital
in the Bosch-brown pools
of Calvin's kin:

shrine-dumb subsoil
in verb-limbs imprisoned
rotting in paradise, reclaimed.

*Lachrima Vecta*

1

Holt-stone, a wreck of ferity,
when will your stare abate?
Heads curve the mist towards him

tomb-glike robes to enecate;
vile raiment, vile raiment
snug for the good of his soul?

Obreption for nothing.

## 2

Lachrymary drought of grace
wordbronze shudder of wing

as shailbreath pierces armour
to labefy *figmentum malum*

in death-dreamed squirts
and thrones of woe.

*Adgestone*

1

Vellum-veil
    curve of guilt.

Ashen moteclaw
    rearing bank.

Wood pierces gut
    nervescape of iron.

    Thread limbering dawn.

2

Swirl of marshpain
      above word-ridge.

Threnody tunes
      its lair

silkthroated
      as iron dyes the water;

cropped of longing
      ribstones speak

and You there
      still wading
           wordpeat with fouled hands
               as Dyer's Spring keens.

*Carisbrooke Castle*

1

Jutes shudder
with frostclaws
swathed in stone
Germania stripping its tribute bare

how many severed heads,
how many bloodbeads
shred fine arteries
mauled imperial moss, livid

your Norman eyes still seeing,
deathwombs, where plough weds state
and mars the teeth to come.

## 2

Pitted sockets scold
the grief of strangely
Saxon fates

headless apotheosis
of bloodworms silting cloud
as decollation's grim floe
seized griefspoils of crown

and misery, sinew-stained,
saunts the cord of spines
until clouds gild in living lines
of molten dead.

## 3

Water-gnawn
the well still breeds
    its ghost

as grave-roots sink
in shell-smoke hoar,
    unasked, brays its hoof

through mounds unknown.

*Arreton Down*

Awl weighs within
    as chalk converts bone

bowels of earth
    secreting bright

the Saxon song
    of dearth and plight

a wreathed goddess of bronze
    approached in spite of blood

an ooze begat before the flood
    their holy circles, their charred stakes.

Cloud's cold clasp
    brines a landscab;

grey, tholes its Muse
    beside us,

as poison-spurts
    raking arms

of burnt clay, dagger-fresh
    cuts of otter bone.

Red deer change:
    I watch the rot-forged clock.

*Arreton Church*

Writhing stone,
lichen hearth,
from clouded crystal

venom smelts
a peering scar.

Torched microliths
of death
where gods of old
gaped;

serenity bent, landless:

angel-shroud
of angled rage.

*St Helens Old Church*

Abreact in bled ruptures.
Nonage of the act. And
in terse flurries you are mourned.
Ogmios hiding the splint's ashen crown

from which ritegnawn words forespawn
the clearing truss of Hildila's gown.

*Binstead Beach*

1

Charred wood-rib alone in sand
where the flown still gather, lending their
hands.

Alders aching with mouthfuls of silt
reaching the shore, to disembark

as waters gnaw as one
and the dead wade deep, refusing to succumb.

## 2

Hoof-timber
acid claims its jaw
shrine-stalked

in the boil of mind

after-birth of toiling rind

root-kiln glowering
the salted floor
as footfalls tempt
the waiting claw.

*Quarr Beach*

Reeds keep watch
as Cistercians sleep,
and men of Stone
drown in clay;

a swirl of agony
greeting the drum
of prayer-midden hawks
lulling depth of rim.

Oak pries its lock for other doors
painting in blood its tabernacle of gore:

leaves read knots
as Benedict cedes
the timber's lot
crowning its prey.

*St Martin's Down*

1

This Christscape of ours
in marrowtears round absent necks
cries on in stayed nearness

gulps of flame-grey suffering
outlasting her fog's mercenary whiteness.

## 2

Wordbarb slights arrears
for graves robbed of insight

craving the magpie's concupiscent ardour

vermiform trust
among voidpearls
turned skeletal.

*Luccombe Chine*

Norse-whet rhythmicide
       the wounds go deep:
             last words from the cross

remembered by all, save the living
       in lichen mounds shrouded
            fellifluous, raw

as Beakers taunt lithic vaticide
       shamed by edges unknown
             to laciniate the brain once more.

*Luccombe Down*

1

Liminal, the barrows mark
the Way of Death,
earthen soul-light
transfixing mounds of rest

where wreaths of leaf and ash
aswarm with singing tusks,
new tongues boring metal,
the furies of ore, to leave
beside the sour nettle

a note refraining sacred doors.

2

Rime-fanged the self stalks
in websplinter blue:

loamhaunt ghosts its horizon
waiting in silence

for epistemicide's clawing ink.

3

Ink-cloven peat
claw your herd red
for to see me disappear

in a chain of flintwounds.

*Bonchurch Landslip*

1

Arm yourself, dendrite
for they would harvest
your light-plumed negations

for the brined lynchets of grief
they prescribe a war god's semen:

nation, state, nemesism
you will not pass the threshold
of this cave.

## 2

Recoil, word,
in roil's surd
glacier of defeat

nought-pawed
the hands mistaken for breath
are less than preferred

by the ones who would eat.

*Bonchurch water spring*

1

Water-shrine, what grows here,
painted on rock, beating a rhythm
confined to treetops?

Garbled in graith of peace,
antler-pierced entropy leavened
the Mist of their Souls

for in swirls the trunks curl
as sacred rains mould and scour the thread,
ancestors moving

through shapes unwed.

## 2

Matter teething into Spirit
as hazel awaits its hand

rocks shelled
from voices felled
at grey and thinning heights

drilling carnyx of glacial veins

waiting for excarnation
god-glimpsed where flint flourished
a thigh, horns calling the unshaped dead

processing eye to eye.

*St. Boniface Down*

Like candles caught
in ignivomous silence
your leaves storm-wrought

figmenting violence
as soiling rage spirals
Godward, and the sole refuge
a moss-gnawn grimace: the pride of Ogham;
the debt of form; the sky
seethes in snowseed sheathed
as naked eyes bleed, a being,
freed, cries.

*Flowers Brook, Ventnor*

1

Threft foci
   gone the cross of dawn

skull's pottery
   lacing modern disease
        with ritestrewn cares
           unsung for millennia

          *Holeweia* keeps the three at bay

    as Norman steel hollows the way
  iron-water born astride the nave
sounding night in the still of day.

2

The silt of amnesia;
blanched encounter
bedding in blood-runes.

A skullvault of leaves nursing refusal
in the prying torture of ersatz light.

Baptised in sight of cliffs
in mines your death a mist
wrought in vaults of ore

to blister, dim, old thaw
and shake the crust of day

at last with death inlaid.

*Steephill Down*

Barbed court
of brinèd horn,
rubescent foal:

dirempt the fatted boar

fulvous lays rest
in the impearling burr
of breath fleeing chest
as ablutions stir
a curse recurs.

*Ventnor Cemetery*

The wounds of Resurrection near
they balk

a flesh of famine their yoke

snapping the lithic cord
for their cancerous grope:

the black-spined eyes
of *agape* scorned

for the vicious hail of state's curving thorn.

*Lowtherville*

Lashen nimbus of ice.
Extolled wordspawn
as powers suffice
the raw Cain's forethorned
archangel of shame.

Forest purrs its torrential curse
as commerce's torrid furs burst
with wings reft of song; herd's
hurt halter, hoar in gauze
in shelter hanged for hollow cause
worming its way
like the Priest on the shore.

*Rew Down*

Tonguethorn
      your cancer is loved
          applauded, ploughed

    in time-scent's fraudulent womb:

out, a thistle-formed glimmer
from which smoke rises
bereft of ritual calm.

*Week Down Barrow Cemetery*

1

Your gulp-cloven air
where feast or famine visit,
you I see pacing

out of poison-grained hoods
disease of recent veneer:

and our steps are purer.

## 2

The sea splices its root
a ribcage fogcleft
a lightdawn that Christ gnaws ripe

and the reft vestige
steals its meat
from silver

as souls thorn His veil.

**3**

Globe-blade entreat
as the burr-shade mnemonics dig

pitying our feeble reach

enduring ice age, technocratic within,
as eyes laid riddling the frost.

4

Tombgnawn, time sleeps
catching the bark
of prayer's brittle heap;

grim brows of deceit
flaying the lash
of time's knowing bleat.

**5**

Prayer-secreted
an oar guides

your flame-famined woe
burnt in heavy grass
mocked by the earthless scent

of times gorged in hellish consent.

*Shippards Chine*

Wordmiddens glow,
death-ocellate,
in the pawed chine
of light-slain night

where gorse wanders its maundering way
sewing its breath in other clay.

Verb-ridden, slow;
iron-fanged chest
mawroot betrothed
to the *bican doene*:

an earthsore laid to rest.

*Apse Wood*

Surd gestation
of the unmourned dead

snow-salt fuscation
the worn eye's
numb thread

with wordsnakes, spark-stricken,
by mercy unshed

as labour retrieves
men unsauced in grace

the aspen's alluvious awe.

*Under a bust of Charles I*

Under a bust of Charles I
men hate Christ
and the last aren't first
as skin-pearls tear themselves
from savage rites

vile unfurling of scar-dirge
screaming its skeletal lust:
you are conquered
and tendons sever.

Lichen-bite, canker-stone,
tender.

*A cellar in the Paris Belleville fauborg, 1871.*

Surface derides occisions
bolted cross-toothed in toil
to soothe none, to see nothing

but adept, painflowered
as sinveils tear

the splinters of ciliary
disease, abattoirs of society

gnashing the spirit's leash.

*For Bram van Velde (1895 – 1981)*

1

You saw the knotted scourge
    and bled

    eyeless soundings
in the shadowgleet thaw

truly yours as the verbscent of Christ
    harrows the door.

2

The wordgoad shocks
Christonyms in flight
as 1647, in lashes of spittle

dredges its soulbile to nought
in facades of avarice
built by nemesistic clowns

not even fit to plough
the famine-soil of propheticide.

3

The verb-risen bleb
recoils its wombshell

        snow-striven,
                apart.

Eyereal, take the dawn,
For your catechists are unwanted here.

# 4

Anguish. Studgnawn waist
corrupt beneath the pulp
of wordslit tongues
feeding in forms of soil

the state-scarred glut
of arterial trust.

*In an Anglican churchyard*

Stylite, your words
will not genuflect
as they torture, again,
the risen Christ –

better unborn than quiescent –

and their wordtithes sink
in brainsoil's night:

what terror before us,
what terror to come.

*For Georges Rouault (1871 – 1958)*

They will walk, they will walk
as the blade cuts Him down
wine devours its cork
ashen dole stains her crown.

Where *Agape* thrives
the State is not
for winds pass by
that ailing moth
enticed to feast
on ravenous rot.

As I stand lost
refusing tear
unbowing ghost's
abyssal cost, transforming fear.

*They will walk, they will walk*
*as the blade cuts Him down*
*wine devours its cork*
*ashen dole stains her crown.*

*'And the angell thrust in his sycle on the erth,
and cut downe the grapes of the vyneyarde off
the erth: and cast them into the grett wynfatt
off the wrath off God, and the wynfatt was
trodden with out the cite...' (Revelation 14:19-
20)*

Time sews its teeth of ice
clinking senescence, the pitch-dark
fall of night

as birds hail in brutal spells
the absonous sough of absinthiate hell
and waters press the grain's dear cloth
as grapes unclot the wine-reft shell
unstalked by plots where Death may dwell

time rues its rank lice
clink of senescent fall
in blood-dark light.

*Hymn to solitude*

I am one
that None will look upon
with tenderness
which leans to touch

You are One
that none will look upon
with thorns crowned, bereaved
a staidness which breathes His trust

It is one
that some will cease to mourn
with bitterness
which frees by touch.

Printed in Great Britain
by Amazon